TWINKLE TWINKLE
Little
Star
do you know how
Loved
YOU ARE

BABY SHOWER FOR:

_____

_____

Stick your favorite
picture here

Guests

Name:_____

Parenting Advice

Wishes for Baby

Resemblance

☐ Mostly Mom   ☐ Definitely Dad

I hope the baby gets Moms:_____

I hope the baby gets Dads:_____

Predictions

Eye Color: _____   Hair Color:_____

Length:_____   Weight:_____

D.O.B:_____   Time:_____

Labor will last: ___Days ___Hours ___Mins

Guests

Name:_____

Parenting Advice

_____
_____
_____
_____
_____

Wishes for Baby

_____
_____
_____
_____
_____

Resemblance

☐ Mostly Mom   ☐ Definitely Dad

I hope the baby gets Moms:_____

I hope the baby gets Dads:_____

Predictions

Eye Color: _____   Hair Color:_____

Length:_____   Weight:_____

D.O.B:_____   Time:_____

Labor will last: ___Days ___Hours ___Mins

Guests

Name:_____

Parenting Advice

Wishes for Baby

Resemblance

☐ Mostly Mom   ☐ Definitely Dad

I hope the baby gets Moms:_____

I hope the baby gets Dads:_____

Predictions

Eye Color: _____   Hair Color:_____

Length:_____   Weight:_____

D.O.B:_____   Time:_____

Labor will last: ___Days ___Hours ___Mins

Guests

Name:_____

Parenting Advice

_____
_____
_____
_____
_____
_____

Wishes for Baby

_____
_____
_____
_____
_____

Resemblance

☐ Mostly Mom   ☐ Definitely Dad

I hope the baby gets Moms:_____

I hope the baby gets Dads:_____

Predictions

Eye Color: _____   Hair Color:_____

Length:_____   Weight:_____

D.O.B:_____   Time:_____

Labor will last: ___Days ___Hours ___Mins

Guests

Name:_____

Parenting Advice

_____
_____
_____
_____
_____
_____

Wishes for Baby

_____
_____
_____
_____
_____
_____

Resemblance

☐ Mostly Mom   ☐ Definitely Dad

I hope the baby gets Moms:_____

I hope the baby gets Dads:_____

Predictions

Eye Color: _____   Hair Color:_____

Length:_____   Weight:_____

D.O.B:_____   Time:_____

Labor will last: ___Days ___Hours ___Mins

Guests

Name:_____

Parenting Advice

_____
_____
_____
_____
_____

Wishes for Baby

_____
_____
_____
_____
_____

Resemblance

☐ Mostly Mom   ☐ Definitely Dad

I hope the baby gets Moms:_____

I hope the baby gets Dads:_____

Predictions

Eye Color: _____   Hair Color:_____

Length:_____   Weight:_____

D.O.B:_____   Time:_____

Labor will last: ___Days ___Hours ___Mins

Guests

Name:_____

Parenting Advice

Wishes for Baby

Resemblance

☐ Mostly Mom   ☐ Definitely Dad

I hope the baby gets Moms:_____

I hope the baby gets Dads:_____

Predictions

Eye Color: _____   Hair Color:_____

Length:_____   Weight:_____

D.O.B:_____   Time:_____

Labor will last: ___Days ___Hours ___Mins

Guests

Name:_____

Parenting Advice

_____
_____
_____
_____
_____
_____

Wishes for Baby

_____
_____
_____
_____
_____
_____

Resemblance

☐ Mostly Mom   ☐ Definitely Dad

I hope the baby gets Moms:_____

I hope the baby gets Dads:_____

Predictions

Eye Color: _____   Hair Color:_____

Length:_____   Weight:_____

D.O.B:_____   Time:_____

Labor will last: ___Days ___Hours ___Mins

Guests

Name:_____

Parenting Advice

Wishes for Baby

Resemblance

☐ Mostly Mom   ☐ Definitely Dad

I hope the baby gets Moms:_____

I hope the baby gets Dads:_____

Predictions

Eye Color: _____   Hair Color:_____

Length:_____   Weight:_____

D.O.B:_____   Time:_____

Labor will last: ___Days ___Hours ___Mins

Guests

Name:_____

Parenting Advice

_____
_____
_____
_____
_____
_____

Wishes for Baby

_____
_____
_____
_____
_____

Resemblance

☐ Mostly Mom   ☐ Definitely Dad

I hope the baby gets Moms:_____

I hope the baby gets Dads:_____

Predictions

Eye Color: _____   Hair Color:_____

Length:_____   Weight:_____

D.O.B:_____   Time:_____

Labor will last: ___Days ___Hours ___Mins

✩✩ Guests ✩✩

Name:_____

✩✩ ✩✩ ✩✩ ✩✩ ✩✩ ✩✩ ✩✩ ✩✩ ✩✩ ✩✩

Parenting Advice

Wishes for Baby

Resemblance

☐ Mostly Mom   ☐ Definitely Dad

I hope the baby gets Moms:_____

I hope the baby gets Dads:_____

Predictions

Eye Color: _____   Hair Color:_____

Length:_____   Weight:_____

D.O.B:_____   Time:_____

Labor will last: ___Days ___Hours ___Mins

Guests

Name:_____

Parenting Advice

_____
_____
_____
_____
_____
_____

Wishes for Baby

_____
_____
_____
_____
_____
_____

Resemblance

☐ Mostly Mom   ☐ Definitely Dad

I hope the baby gets Moms:_____

I hope the baby gets Dads:_____

Predictions

Eye Color: _____   Hair Color:_____

Length:_____   Weight:_____

D.O.B:_____   Time:_____

Labor will last: ___Days ___Hours ___Mins

Guests

Name:_____

Parenting Advice

_____
_____
_____
_____
_____
_____

Wishes for Baby

_____
_____
_____
_____
_____

Resemblance

☐ Mostly Mom   ☐ Definitely Dad

I hope the baby gets Moms:_____

I hope the baby gets Dads:_____

Predictions

Eye Color: _____   Hair Color:_____

Length:_____   Weight:_____

D.O.B:_____   Time:_____

Labor will last: ___Days ___Hours ___Mins

Guests

Name:_____

Parenting Advice

_____
_____
_____
_____
_____
_____

Wishes for Baby

_____
_____
_____
_____
_____

Resemblance

☐ Mostly Mom   ☐ Definitely Dad

I hope the baby gets Moms:_____

I hope the baby gets Dads:_____

Predictions

Eye Color: _____   Hair Color:_____

Length:_____   Weight:_____

D.O.B:_____   Time:_____

Labor will last: ___Days ___Hours ___Mins

Guests

Name:_____

Parenting Advice

Wishes for Baby

Resemblance

☐ Mostly Mom   ☐ Definitely Dad

I hope the baby gets Moms:_____

I hope the baby gets Dads:_____

Predictions

Eye Color: _____   Hair Color:_____

Length:_____   Weight:_____

D.O.B:_____   Time:_____

Labor will last: ___Days ___Hours ___Mins

Guests

Name:_____

Parenting Advice

_____
_____
_____
_____
_____
_____

Wishes for Baby

_____
_____
_____
_____
_____
_____

Resemblance

☐ Mostly Mom   ☐ Definitely Dad

I hope the baby gets Moms:_____

I hope the baby gets Dads:_____

Predictions

Eye Color: _____   Hair Color:_____

Length:_____   Weight:_____

D.O.B:_____   Time:_____

Labor will last: ___Days ___Hours ___Mins

Guests

Name:_____

Parenting Advice

Wishes for Baby

Resemblance

☐ Mostly Mom   ☐ Definitely Dad

I hope the baby gets Moms:_____

I hope the baby gets Dads:_____

Predictions

Eye Color: _____   Hair Color:_____

Length:_____   Weight:_____

D.O.B:_____   Time:_____

Labor will last: ___Days ___Hours ___Mins

Guests

Name:_____

Parenting Advice

Wishes for Baby

Resemblance

☐ Mostly Mom   ☐ Definitely Dad

I hope the baby gets Moms:_____

I hope the baby gets Dads:_____

Predictions

Eye Color: _____   Hair Color:_____

Length:_____   Weight:_____

D.O.B:_____   Time:_____

Labor will last: ___Days ___Hours ___Mins

Guests

Name:_____

Parenting Advice

Wishes for Baby

Resemblance

☐ Mostly Mom   ☐ Definitely Dad

I hope the baby gets Moms:_____

I hope the baby gets Dads:_____

Predictions

Eye Color: _____   Hair Color:_____

Length:_____   Weight:_____

D.O.B:_____   Time:_____

Labor will last: ___Days ___Hours ___Mins

Guests

Name:_____

Parenting Advice

_____
_____
_____
_____
_____
_____

Wishes for Baby

_____
_____
_____
_____
_____
_____

Resemblance

☐ Mostly Mom   ☐ Definitely Dad

I hope the baby gets Moms:_____

I hope the baby gets Dads:_____

Predictions

Eye Color: _____   Hair Color:_____

Length:_____   Weight:_____

D.O.B:_____   Time:_____

Labor will last: ___Days ___Hours ___Mins

Guests

Name:_____

Parenting Advice

_____
_____
_____
_____
_____
_____

Wishes for Baby

_____
_____
_____
_____
_____
_____

Resemblance

☐ Mostly Mom   ☐ Definitely Dad

I hope the baby gets Moms:_____

I hope the baby gets Dads:_____

Predictions

Eye Color: _____   Hair Color:_____

Length:_____   Weight:_____

D.O.B:_____   Time:_____

Labor will last: ___Days ___Hours ___Mins

Guests

Name:_____

Parenting Advice

_____
_____
_____
_____
_____

Wishes for Baby

_____
_____
_____
_____
_____

Resemblance

☐ Mostly Mom   ☐ Definitely Dad

I hope the baby gets Moms:_____

I hope the baby gets Dads:_____

Predictions

Eye Color: _____   Hair Color:_____

Length:_____   Weight:_____

D.O.B:_____   Time:_____

Labor will last: ___Days ___Hours ___Mins

Guests

Name:_____

Parenting Advice

_____
_____
_____
_____
_____
_____

Wishes for Baby

_____
_____
_____
_____
_____
_____

Resemblance

☐ Mostly Mom   ☐ Definitely Dad

I hope the baby gets Moms:_____

I hope the baby gets Dads:_____

Predictions

Eye Color: _____   Hair Color:_____

Length:_____   Weight:_____

D.O.B:_____   Time:_____

Labor will last: ___Days ___Hours ___Mins

Guests

Name:_____

Parenting Advice

_____
_____
_____
_____
_____
_____

Wishes for Baby

_____
_____
_____
_____
_____
_____

Resemblance

☐ Mostly Mom   ☐ Definitely Dad

I hope the baby gets Moms:_____

I hope the baby gets Dads:_____

Predictions

Eye Color: _____   Hair Color:_____

Length:_____   Weight:_____

D.O.B:_____   Time:_____

Labor will last: ___Days ___Hours ___Mins

Guests

Name:_____

Parenting Advice

_____
_____
_____
_____
_____
_____

Wishes for Baby

_____
_____
_____
_____
_____
_____

Resemblance

☐ Mostly Mom   ☐ Definitely Dad

I hope the baby gets Moms:_____

I hope the baby gets Dads:_____

Predictions

Eye Color: _____   Hair Color:_____

Length:_____   Weight:_____

D.O.B:_____   Time:_____

Labor will last: ___Days ___Hours ___Mins

Guests

Name:_____

Parenting Advice

_____
_____
_____
_____
_____
_____

Wishes for Baby

_____
_____
_____
_____
_____

Resemblance

☐ Mostly Mom   ☐ Definitely Dad

I hope the baby gets Moms:_____

I hope the baby gets Dads:_____

Predictions

Eye Color: _____   Hair Color:_____

Length:_____   Weight:_____

D.O.B:_____   Time:_____

Labor will last: ___Days ___Hours ___Mins

Guests

Name:_____

Parenting Advice

Wishes for Baby

Resemblance

☐ Mostly Mom   ☐ Definitely Dad

I hope the baby gets Moms:_____

I hope the baby gets Dads:_____

Predictions

Eye Color: _____   Hair Color:_____

Length:_____   Weight:_____

D.O.B:_____   Time:_____

Labor will last: ___Days ___Hours ___Mins

Guests

Name:_____

Parenting Advice

_____
_____
_____
_____
_____
_____

Wishes for Baby

_____
_____
_____
_____
_____

Resemblance

☐ Mostly Mom   ☐ Definitely Dad

I hope the baby gets Moms:_____

I hope the baby gets Dads:_____

Predictions

Eye Color: _____   Hair Color:_____

Length:_____   Weight:_____

D.O.B:_____   Time:_____

Labor will last: ___Days ___Hours ___Mins

Guests

Name:_____

Parenting Advice

_____
_____
_____
_____
_____
_____

Wishes for Baby

_____
_____
_____
_____
_____
_____

Resemblance

☐ Mostly Mom   ☐ Definitely Dad

I hope the baby gets Moms:_____

I hope the baby gets Dads:_____

Predictions

Eye Color: _____   Hair Color:_____

Length:_____   Weight:_____

D.O.B:_____   Time:_____

Labor will last: ___Days ___Hours ___Mins

Guests

Name:_____

Parenting Advice

_____
_____
_____
_____
_____
_____

Wishes for Baby

_____
_____
_____
_____
_____

Resemblance

☐ Mostly Mom   ☐ Definitely Dad

I hope the baby gets Moms:_____

I hope the baby gets Dads:_____

Predictions

Eye Color: _____   Hair Color:_____

Length:_____   Weight:_____

D.O.B:_____   Time:_____

Labor will last: ___Days ___Hours ___Mins

Guests

Name:_____

Parenting Advice

Wishes for Baby

Resemblance

☐ Mostly Mom   ☐ Definitely Dad

I hope the baby gets Moms:_____

I hope the baby gets Dads:_____

Predictions

Eye Color: _____   Hair Color:_____

Length:_____   Weight:_____

D.O.B:_____   Time:_____

Labor will last: ___Days ___Hours ___Mins

Guests

Name:_____

Parenting Advice

_____
_____
_____
_____
_____
_____

Wishes for Baby

_____
_____
_____
_____
_____
_____

Resemblance

☐ Mostly Mom   ☐ Definitely Dad

I hope the baby gets Moms:_____

I hope the baby gets Dads:_____

Predictions

Eye Color: _____   Hair Color:_____

Length:_____   Weight:_____

D.O.B:_____   Time:_____

Labor will last: ___Days ___Hours ___Mins

Guests

Name:_____

Parenting Advice

_____
_____
_____
_____
_____
_____

Wishes for Baby

_____
_____
_____
_____
_____
_____

Resemblance

☐ Mostly Mom   ☐ Definitely Dad

I hope the baby gets Moms:_____

I hope the baby gets Dads:_____

Predictions

Eye Color: _____   Hair Color:_____

Length:_____   Weight:_____

D.O.B:_____   Time:_____

Labor will last: ___Days ___Hours ___Mins

Guests

Name:_____

Parenting Advice

_____
_____
_____
_____
_____
_____

Wishes for Baby

_____
_____
_____
_____
_____
_____

Resemblance

☐ Mostly Mom   ☐ Definitely Dad

I hope the baby gets Moms:_____

I hope the baby gets Dads:_____

Predictions

Eye Color: _____   Hair Color:_____

Length:_____   Weight:_____

D.O.B:_____   Time:_____

Labor will last: ___Days ___Hours ___Mins

 Guests

Name:_____

Parenting Advice

Wishes for Baby

Resemblance

☐ Mostly Mom   ☐ Definitely Dad

I hope the baby gets Moms:_____

I hope the baby gets Dads:_____

Predictions

Eye Color: _____   Hair Color:_____

Length:_____   Weight:_____

D.O.B:_____   Time:_____

Labor will last: ___Days ___Hours ___Mins

Guests

Name:_____

Parenting Advice

Wishes for Baby

Resemblance

☐ Mostly Mom   ☐ Definitely Dad

I hope the baby gets Moms:_____

I hope the baby gets Dads:_____

Predictions

Eye Color: _____   Hair Color:_____

Length:_____   Weight:_____

D.O.B:_____   Time:_____

Labor will last: ___Days ___Hours ___Mins

Guests

Name:_____

Parenting Advice

_____
_____
_____
_____
_____
_____

Wishes for Baby

_____
_____
_____
_____
_____
_____

Resemblance

☐ Mostly Mom   ☐ Definitely Dad

I hope the baby gets Moms:_____

I hope the baby gets Dads:_____

Predictions

Eye Color: _____   Hair Color:_____

Length:_____   Weight:_____

D.O.B:_____   Time:_____

Labor will last: ___Days ___Hours ___Mins

Guests

Name:_____

Parenting Advice

_____
_____
_____
_____
_____
_____

Wishes for Baby

_____
_____
_____
_____
_____
_____

Resemblance

☐ Mostly Mom   ☐ Definitely Dad

I hope the baby gets Moms:_____

I hope the baby gets Dads:_____

Predictions

Eye Color: _____   Hair Color:_____

Length:_____   Weight:_____

D.O.B:_____   Time:_____

Labor will last: ___Days ___Hours ___Mins

Guests

Name:_____

Parenting Advice

Wishes for Baby

Resemblance

☐ Mostly Mom   ☐ Definitely Dad

I hope the baby gets Moms:_____

I hope the baby gets Dads:_____

Predictions

Eye Color: _____   Hair Color:_____

Length:_____   Weight:_____

D.O.B:_____   Time:_____

Labor will last: ___Days ___Hours ___Mins

Guests

Name:_____

Parenting Advice

_____
_____
_____
_____
_____
_____

Wishes for Baby

_____
_____
_____
_____
_____
_____

Resemblance

☐ Mostly Mom   ☐ Definitely Dad

I hope the baby gets Moms:_____

I hope the baby gets Dads:_____

Predictions

Eye Color: _____   Hair Color:_____

Length:_____   Weight:_____

D.O.B:_____   Time:_____

Labor will last: ___Days ___Hours ___Mins

Guests

Name:_____

Parenting Advice

_____
_____
_____
_____
_____
_____

Wishes for Baby

_____
_____
_____
_____
_____
_____

Resemblance

☐ Mostly Mom   ☐ Definitely Dad

I hope the baby gets Moms:_____

I hope the baby gets Dads:_____

Predictions

Eye Color: _____   Hair Color:_____

Length:_____   Weight:_____

D.O.B:_____   Time:_____

Labor will last: ___Days ___Hours ___Mins

Guests

Name:_____

Parenting Advice

_____
_____
_____
_____
_____
_____

Wishes for Baby

_____
_____
_____
_____
_____
_____

Resemblance

☐ Mostly Mom   ☐ Definitely Dad

I hope the baby gets Moms:_____

I hope the baby gets Dads:_____

Predictions

Eye Color: _____   Hair Color:_____

Length:_____   Weight:_____

D.O.B:_____   Time:_____

Labor will last: ___Days ___Hours ___Mins

Guests

Name:_____

Parenting Advice

_____
_____
_____
_____
_____
_____

Wishes for Baby

_____
_____
_____
_____
_____
_____

Resemblance

☐ Mostly Mom   ☐ Definitely Dad

I hope the baby gets Moms:_____

I hope the baby gets Dads:_____

Predictions

Eye Color: _____   Hair Color:_____

Length:_____   Weight:_____

D.O.B:_____   Time:_____

Labor will last: ___Days ___Hours ___Mins

Guests

Name:_____

Parenting Advice

Wishes for Baby

Resemblance

☐ Mostly Mom   ☐ Definitely Dad

I hope the baby gets Moms:_____

I hope the baby gets Dads:_____

Predictions

Eye Color: _____   Hair Color:_____

Length:_____   Weight:_____

D.O.B:_____   Time:_____

Labor will last: ___Days ___Hours ___Mins

Guests

Name:_____

Parenting Advice

_____
_____
_____
_____
_____
_____

Wishes for Baby

_____
_____
_____
_____
_____

Resemblance

☐ Mostly Mom   ☐ Definitely Dad

I hope the baby gets Moms:_____

I hope the baby gets Dads:_____

Predictions

Eye Color: _____   Hair Color:_____

Length:_____   Weight:_____

D.O.B:_____   Time:_____

Labor will last: ___Days ___Hours ___Mins

Guests

Name:_____

Parenting Advice

_____
_____
_____
_____
_____
_____

Wishes for Baby

_____
_____
_____
_____
_____
_____

Resemblance

☐ Mostly Mom   ☐ Definitely Dad

I hope the baby gets Moms:_____

I hope the baby gets Dads:_____

Predictions

Eye Color: _____   Hair Color:_____

Length:_____   Weight:_____

D.O.B:_____   Time:_____

Labor will last: ___Days ___Hours ___Mins

Guests

Name:_____

Parenting Advice

_____
_____
_____
_____
_____
_____

Wishes for Baby

_____
_____
_____
_____
_____
_____

Resemblance

☐ Mostly Mom   ☐ Definitely Dad

I hope the baby gets Moms:_____

I hope the baby gets Dads:_____

Predictions

Eye Color: _____   Hair Color:_____

Length:_____   Weight:_____

D.O.B:_____   Time:_____

Labor will last: ___Days ___Hours ___Mins

Guests

Name:_____

Parenting Advice

_____
_____
_____
_____
_____
_____

Wishes for Baby

_____
_____
_____
_____
_____

Resemblance

☐ Mostly Mom   ☐ Definitely Dad

I hope the baby gets Moms:_____

I hope the baby gets Dads:_____

Predictions

Eye Color: _____   Hair Color:_____

Length:_____   Weight:_____

D.O.B:_____   Time:_____

Labor will last: ___Days ___Hours ___Mins

Guests

Name:_____

Parenting Advice

Wishes for Baby

Resemblance

☐ Mostly Mom   ☐ Definitely Dad

I hope the baby gets Moms:_____

I hope the baby gets Dads:_____

Predictions

Eye Color: _____   Hair Color:_____

Length:_____   Weight:_____

D.O.B:_____   Time:_____

Labor will last: ___Days ___Hours ___Mins

Guests

Name:_____

Parenting Advice

_ _
_ _
_ _
_ _
_ _
_ _

Wishes for Baby

_ _
_ _
_ _
_ _
_ _

Resemblance

☐ Mostly Mom   ☐ Definitely Dad

I hope the baby gets Moms:_____

I hope the baby gets Dads:_____

Predictions

Eye Color: _____   Hair Color:_____

Length:_____   Weight:_____

D.O.B:_____   Time:_____

Labor will last: ___Days ___Hours ___Mins

Guests

Name:_____

Parenting Advice

Wishes for Baby

Resemblance

☐ Mostly Mom   ☐ Definitely Dad

I hope the baby gets Moms:_____

I hope the baby gets Dads:_____

Predictions

Eye Color: _____   Hair Color:_____

Length:_____   Weight:_____

D.O.B:_____   Time:_____

Labor will last: ___Days ___Hours ___Mins

Guests

Name:_____

Parenting Advice

Wishes for Baby

Resemblance

☐ Mostly Mom   ☐ Definitely Dad

I hope the baby gets Moms:_____

I hope the baby gets Dads:_____

Predictions

Eye Color: _____   Hair Color:_____

Length:_____   Weight:_____

D.O.B:_____   Time:_____

Labor will last: ___Days ___Hours ___Mins

Guests

Name:_____

Parenting Advice

_____
_____
_____
_____
_____
_____

Wishes for Baby

_____
_____
_____
_____
_____
_____

Resemblance

☐ Mostly Mom   ☐ Definitely Dad

I hope the baby gets Moms:_____

I hope the baby gets Dads:_____

Predictions

Eye Color: _____   Hair Color:_____

Length:_____   Weight:_____

D.O.B:_____   Time:_____

Labor will last: ___Days ___Hours ___Mins

Guests

Name:_____

Parenting Advice

_____
_____
_____
_____
_____
_____

Wishes for Baby

_____
_____
_____
_____
_____
_____

Resemblance

☐ Mostly Mom   ☐ Definitely Dad

I hope the baby gets Moms:_____

I hope the baby gets Dads:_____

Predictions

Eye Color: _____   Hair Color:_____

Length:_____   Weight:_____

D.O.B:_____   Time:_____

Labor will last: ___Days ___Hours ___Mins

Guests

Name:_____

Parenting Advice

_____
_____
_____
_____
_____
_____

Wishes for Baby

_____
_____
_____
_____
_____
_____

Resemblance

☐ Mostly Mom   ☐ Definitely Dad

I hope the baby gets Moms:_____

I hope the baby gets Dads:_____

Predictions

Eye Color: _____   Hair Color:_____

Length:_____   Weight:_____

D.O.B:_____   Time:_____

Labor will last: ___Days ___Hours ___Mins

Guests

Name:_____

Parenting Advice

_____
_____
_____
_____
_____
_____

Wishes for Baby

_____
_____
_____
_____
_____
_____

Resemblance

☐ Mostly Mom   ☐ Definitely Dad

I hope the baby gets Moms:_____

I hope the baby gets Dads:_____

Predictions

Eye Color: _____   Hair Color:_____

Length:_____   Weight:_____

D.O.B:_____   Time:_____

Labor will last: ___Days ___Hours ___Mins

Guests

Name:_____

Parenting Advice

_____
_____
_____
_____
_____

Wishes for Baby

_____
_____
_____
_____
_____

Resemblance

☐ Mostly Mom   ☐ Definitely Dad

I hope the baby gets Moms:_____

I hope the baby gets Dads:_____

Predictions

Eye Color: _____   Hair Color:_____

Length:_____   Weight:_____

D.O.B:_____   Time:_____

Labor will last: ___Days ___Hours ___Mins

Guests

Name:_____

Parenting Advice

_____
_____
_____
_____
_____

Wishes for Baby

_____
_____
_____
_____
_____

Resemblance

☐ Mostly Mom   ☐ Definitely Dad

I hope the baby gets Moms:_____

I hope the baby gets Dads:_____

Predictions

Eye Color: _____   Hair Color:_____

Length:_____   Weight:_____

D.O.B:_____   Time:_____

Labor will last: ___Days ___Hours ___Mins

Guests

Name:_____

Parenting Advice

Wishes for Baby

Resemblance

☐ Mostly Mom   ☐ Definitely Dad

I hope the baby gets Moms:_____

I hope the baby gets Dads:_____

Predictions

Eye Color: _____   Hair Color:_____

Length:_____   Weight:_____

D.O.B:_____   Time:_____

Labor will last: ___Days ___Hours ___Mins

Guests

Name:_____

Parenting Advice

_____

_____

_____

_____

_____

_____

Wishes for Baby

_____

_____

_____

_____

_____

Resemblance

☐ Mostly Mom   ☐ Definitely Dad

I hope the baby gets Moms:_____

I hope the baby gets Dads:_____

Predictions

Eye Color: _____   Hair Color:_____

Length:_____   Weight:_____

D.O.B:_____   Time:_____

Labor will last: ___Days ___Hours ___Mins

Guests

Name:_____

Parenting Advice

_____
_____
_____
_____
_____
_____

Wishes for Baby

_____
_____
_____
_____
_____
_____

Resemblance

☐ Mostly Mom   ☐ Definitely Dad

I hope the baby gets Moms:_____

I hope the baby gets Dads:_____

Predictions

Eye Color: _____   Hair Color:_____

Length:_____   Weight:_____

D.O.B:_____   Time:_____

Labor will last: ___Days ___Hours ___Mins

Guests

Name:_____

Parenting Advice

_____
_____
_____
_____
_____

Wishes for Baby

_____
_____
_____
_____
_____

Resemblance

☐ Mostly Mom   ☐ Definitely Dad

I hope the baby gets Moms:_____

I hope the baby gets Dads:_____

Predictions

Eye Color: _____   Hair Color:_____

Length:_____   Weight:_____

D.O.B:_____   Time:_____

Labor will last: ___Days ___Hours ___Mins

Guests

Name:_____

Parenting Advice

_____
_____
_____
_____
_____
_____

Wishes for Baby

_____
_____
_____
_____
_____
_____

Resemblance

☐ Mostly Mom   ☐ Definitely Dad

I hope the baby gets Moms:_____

I hope the baby gets Dads:_____

Predictions

Eye Color: _____   Hair Color:_____

Length:_____   Weight:_____

D.O.B:_____   Time:_____

Labor will last: ___Days ___Hours ___Mins

Guests

Name:_____

Parenting Advice

_____
_____
_____
_____
_____
_____

Wishes for Baby

_____
_____
_____
_____
_____

Resemblance

☐ Mostly Mom   ☐ Definitely Dad

I hope the baby gets Moms:_____

I hope the baby gets Dads:_____

Predictions

Eye Color: _____   Hair Color:_____

Length:_____   Weight:_____

D.O.B:_____   Time:_____

Labor will last: ___Days ___Hours ___Mins

Guests

Name:_____

Parenting Advice

_____
_____
_____
_____
_____
_____

Wishes for Baby

_____
_____
_____
_____
_____
_____

Resemblance

☐ Mostly Mom   ☐ Definitely Dad

I hope the baby gets Moms:_____

I hope the baby gets Dads:_____

Predictions

Eye Color: _____   Hair Color:_____

Length:_____   Weight:_____

D.O.B:_____   Time:_____

Labor will last: ___Days ___Hours ___Mins

Guests

Name:_____

Parenting Advice

- -
- -
- -
- -
- -
- -

Wishes for Baby

- -
- -
- -
- -
- -

Resemblance

☐ Mostly Mom   ☐ Definitely Dad

I hope the baby gets Moms:_____

I hope the baby gets Dads:_____

Predictions

Eye Color: _____   Hair Color:_____

Length:_____   Weight:_____

D.O.B:_____   Time:_____

Labor will last: ___Days ___Hours ___Mins

Guests

Name:_____

Parenting Advice

Wishes for Baby

Resemblance

☐ Mostly Mom   ☐ Definitely Dad

I hope the baby gets Moms:_____

I hope the baby gets Dads:_____

Predictions

Eye Color: _____   Hair Color:_____

Length:_____   Weight:_____

D.O.B:_____   Time:_____

Labor will last: ___Days ___Hours ___Mins

Guests

Name:_____

Parenting Advice

Wishes for Baby

Resemblance

☐ Mostly Mom   ☐ Definitely Dad

I hope the baby gets Moms:_____

I hope the baby gets Dads:_____

Predictions

Eye Color: _____   Hair Color:_____

Length:_____   Weight:_____

D.O.B:_____   Time:_____

Labor will last: ___Days ___Hours ___Mins

Guests

Name:_____

Parenting Advice

Wishes for Baby

Resemblance

☐ Mostly Mom   ☐ Definitely Dad

I hope the baby gets Moms:_____

I hope the baby gets Dads:_____

Predictions

Eye Color: _____   Hair Color:_____

Length:_____   Weight:_____

D.O.B:_____   Time:_____

Labor will last: ___Days ___Hours ___Mins

Guests

Name:_____

Parenting Advice

_____
_____
_____
_____
_____
_____

Wishes for Baby

_____
_____
_____
_____
_____

Resemblance

☐ Mostly Mom   ☐ Definitely Dad

I hope the baby gets Moms:_____

I hope the baby gets Dads:_____

Predictions

Eye Color: _____   Hair Color:_____

Length:_____   Weight:_____

D.O.B:_____   Time:_____

Labor will last: ___Days ___Hours ___Mins

Guests

Name:_____

Parenting Advice

Wishes for Baby

Resemblance

☐ Mostly Mom   ☐ Definitely Dad

I hope the baby gets Moms:_____

I hope the baby gets Dads:_____

Predictions

Eye Color: _____   Hair Color:_____

Length:_____   Weight:_____

D.O.B:_____   Time:_____

Labor will last: ___Days ___Hours ___Mins

Guests

Name:_____

Parenting Advice

- -
- -
- -
- -
- -
- -

Wishes for Baby

- -
- -
- -
- -
- -

Resemblance

☐ Mostly Mom   ☐ Definitely Dad

I hope the baby gets Moms:_____

I hope the baby gets Dads:_____

Predictions

Eye Color: _____   Hair Color:_____

Length:_____   Weight:_____

D.O.B:_____   Time:_____

Labor will last: ___Days ___Hours ___Mins

Guests

Name:_____

Parenting Advice

_____
_____
_____
_____
_____
_____

Wishes for Baby

_____
_____
_____
_____
_____
_____

Resemblance

☐ Mostly Mom   ☐ Definitely Dad

I hope the baby gets Moms:_____

I hope the baby gets Dads:_____

Predictions

Eye Color: _____   Hair Color:_____

Length:_____   Weight:_____

D.O.B:_____   Time:_____

Labor will last: ___Days ___Hours ___Mins

Guests

Name:_____

Parenting Advice

_____
_____
_____
_____
_____
_____

Wishes for Baby

_____
_____
_____
_____
_____
_____

Resemblance

☐ Mostly Mom   ☐ Definitely Dad

I hope the baby gets Moms:_____

I hope the baby gets Dads:_____

Predictions

Eye Color: _____   Hair Color:_____

Length:_____   Weight:_____

D.O.B:_____   Time:_____

Labor will last: ___Days ___Hours ___Mins

Guests

Name:_____

Parenting Advice

_____
_____
_____
_____
_____
_____

Wishes for Baby

_____
_____
_____
_____
_____

Resemblance

☐ Mostly Mom   ☐ Definitely Dad

I hope the baby gets Moms:_____

I hope the baby gets Dads:_____

Predictions

Eye Color: _____   Hair Color:_____

Length:_____   Weight:_____

D.O.B:_____   Time:_____

Labor will last: ___Days ___Hours ___Mins

Guests

Name:_____

Parenting Advice

_____
_____
_____
_____
_____
_____

Wishes for Baby

_____
_____
_____
_____
_____

Resemblance

☐ Mostly Mom   ☐ Definitely Dad

I hope the baby gets Moms:_____

I hope the baby gets Dads:_____

Predictions

Eye Color: _____   Hair Color:_____

Length:_____   Weight:_____

D.O.B:_____   Time:_____

Labor will last: ___Days ___Hours ___Mins

Guests

Name:_____

Parenting Advice

_____
_____
_____
_____
_____
_____

Wishes for Baby

_____
_____
_____
_____
_____
_____

Resemblance

☐ Mostly Mom   ☐ Definitely Dad

I hope the baby gets Moms:_____

I hope the baby gets Dads:_____

Predictions

Eye Color: _____   Hair Color:_____

Length:_____   Weight:_____

D.O.B:_____   Time:_____

Labor will last: ___Days ___Hours ___Mins

Guests

Name:_____

Parenting Advice

_____
_____
_____
_____
_____
_____

Wishes for Baby

_____
_____
_____
_____
_____
_____

Resemblance

☐ Mostly Mom   ☐ Definitely Dad

I hope the baby gets Moms:_____

I hope the baby gets Dads:_____

Predictions

Eye Color: _____   Hair Color:_____

Length:_____   Weight:_____

D.O.B:_____   Time:_____

Labor will last: ___Days ___Hours ___Mins

Guests

Name:_____

Parenting Advice

_____
_____
_____
_____
_____
_____

Wishes for Baby

_____
_____
_____
_____
_____
_____

Resemblance

☐ Mostly Mom   ☐ Definitely Dad

I hope the baby gets Moms:_____

I hope the baby gets Dads:_____

Predictions

Eye Color: _____   Hair Color:_____

Length:_____   Weight:_____

D.O.B:_____   Time:_____

Labor will last: ___Days ___Hours ___Mins

Guests

Name:_____

Parenting Advice

_____
_____
_____
_____
_____
_____

Wishes for Baby

_____
_____
_____
_____
_____
_____

Resemblance

☐ Mostly Mom   ☐ Definitely Dad

I hope the baby gets Moms:_____

I hope the baby gets Dads:_____

Predictions

Eye Color: _____   Hair Color:_____

Length:_____   Weight:_____

D.O.B:_____   Time:_____

Labor will last: ___Days ___Hours ___Mins

✩✩ Guests ✩✩

Name:_____

✩✩ ✩✩ ✩✩ ✩✩ ✩✩ ✩✩ ✩✩ ✩✩ ✩✩ ✩✩

Parenting Advice

_____
_____
_____
_____
_____
_____

Wishes for Baby

_____
_____
_____
_____
_____
_____

Resemblance

☐ Mostly Mom   ☐ Definitely Dad

I hope the baby gets Moms:_____

I hope the baby gets Dads:_____

Predictions

Eye Color: _____   Hair Color:_____

Length:_____   Weight:_____

D.O.B:_____   Time:_____

Labor will last: ___Days ___Hours ___Mins

Guests

Name:_____

Parenting Advice

_____
_____
_____
_____
_____
_____

Wishes for Baby

_____
_____
_____
_____
_____
_____

Resemblance

☐ Mostly Mom   ☐ Definitely Dad

I hope the baby gets Moms:_____

I hope the baby gets Dads:_____

Predictions

Eye Color: _____   Hair Color:_____

Length:_____   Weight:_____

D.O.B:_____   Time:_____

Labor will last: ___Days ___Hours ___Mins

Guests

Name:_____

Parenting Advice

Wishes for Baby

Resemblance

☐ Mostly Mom   ☐ Definitely Dad

I hope the baby gets Moms:_____

I hope the baby gets Dads:_____

Predictions

Eye Color: _____   Hair Color:_____

Length:_____   Weight:_____

D.O.B:_____   Time:_____

Labor will last: ___Days ___Hours ___Mins

Guests

Name:_____

Parenting Advice

_____

_____

_____

_____

_____

_____

Wishes for Baby

_____

_____

_____

_____

_____

_____

Resemblance

☐ Mostly Mom   ☐ Definitely Dad

I hope the baby gets Moms:_____

I hope the baby gets Dads:_____

Predictions

Eye Color: _____   Hair Color:_____

Length:_____   Weight:_____

D.O.B:_____   Time:_____

Labor will last: ___Days ___Hours ___Mins

Guests

Name:_____

Parenting Advice

_____
_____
_____
_____
_____
_____

Wishes for Baby

_____
_____
_____
_____
_____
_____

Resemblance

☐ Mostly Mom   ☐ Definitely Dad

I hope the baby gets Moms:_____

I hope the baby gets Dads:_____

Predictions

Eye Color: _____   Hair Color:_____

Length:_____   Weight:_____

D.O.B:_____   Time:_____

Labor will last: ___Days ___Hours ___Mins

Guests

Name:_____

Parenting Advice

_____
_____
_____
_____
_____
_____

Wishes for Baby

_____
_____
_____
_____
_____

Resemblance

☐ Mostly Mom   ☐ Definitely Dad

I hope the baby gets Moms:_____

I hope the baby gets Dads:_____

Predictions

Eye Color: _____   Hair Color:_____

Length:_____   Weight:_____

D.O.B:_____   Time:_____

Labor will last: ___Days ___Hours ___Mins

Guests

Name:_____

Parenting Advice

_____
_____
_____
_____
_____
_____

Wishes for Baby

_____
_____
_____
_____
_____
_____

Resemblance

☐ Mostly Mom   ☐ Definitely Dad

I hope the baby gets Moms:_____

I hope the baby gets Dads:_____

Predictions

Eye Color: _____   Hair Color:_____

Length:_____   Weight:_____

D.O.B:_____   Time:_____

Labor will last: ___Days ___Hours ___Mins

Guests

Name:_____

Parenting Advice

_____
_____
_____
_____
_____
_____

Wishes for Baby

_____
_____
_____
_____
_____

Resemblance

☐ Mostly Mom   ☐ Definitely Dad

I hope the baby gets Moms:_____

I hope the baby gets Dads:_____

Predictions

Eye Color: _____   Hair Color:_____

Length:_____   Weight:_____

D.O.B:_____   Time:_____

Labor will last: ___Days ___Hours ___Mins

Guests

Name:_____

Parenting Advice

_____

_____

_____

_____

_____

_____

Wishes for Baby

_____

_____

_____

_____

_____

Resemblance

☐ Mostly Mom   ☐ Definitely Dad

I hope the baby gets Moms:_____

I hope the baby gets Dads:_____

Predictions

Eye Color: _____   Hair Color:_____

Length:_____   Weight:_____

D.O.B:_____   Time:_____

Labor will last: ___Days ___Hours ___Mins

Guests

Name:_____

Parenting Advice

- -
- -
- -
- -
- -

Wishes for Baby

- -
- -
- -
- -
- -

Resemblance

☐ Mostly Mom   ☐ Definitely Dad

I hope the baby gets Moms:_____

I hope the baby gets Dads:_____

Predictions

Eye Color: _____   Hair Color:_____

Length:_____   Weight:_____

D.O.B:_____   Time:_____

Labor will last: ___Days ___Hours ___Mins

Guests

Name:_____

Parenting Advice

_____
_____
_____
_____
_____

Wishes for Baby

_____
_____
_____
_____
_____

Resemblance

☐ Mostly Mom   ☐ Definitely Dad

I hope the baby gets Moms:_____

I hope the baby gets Dads:_____

Predictions

Eye Color: _____   Hair Color:_____

Length:_____   Weight:_____

D.O.B:_____   Time:_____

Labor will last: ___Days ___Hours ___Mins

Guests

Name:_____

Parenting Advice

_____
_____
_____
_____
_____
_____

Wishes for Baby

_____
_____
_____
_____
_____
_____

Resemblance

☐ Mostly Mom   ☐ Definitely Dad

I hope the baby gets Moms:_____

I hope the baby gets Dads:_____

Predictions

Eye Color: _____   Hair Color:_____

Length:_____   Weight:_____

D.O.B:_____   Time:_____

Labor will last: ___Days ___Hours ___Mins

Guests

Name:_____

Parenting Advice

_____
_____
_____
_____
_____
_____

Wishes for Baby

_____
_____
_____
_____
_____
_____

Resemblance

☐ Mostly Mom   ☐ Definitely Dad

I hope the baby gets Moms:_____

I hope the baby gets Dads:_____

Predictions

Eye Color: _____   Hair Color:_____

Length:_____   Weight:_____

D.O.B:_____   Time:_____

Labor will last: ___Days ___Hours ___Mins

Guests

Name:_____

Parenting Advice

_____
_____
_____
_____
_____
_____

Wishes for Baby

_____
_____
_____
_____
_____

Resemblance

☐ Mostly Mom   ☐ Definitely Dad

I hope the baby gets Moms:_____

I hope the baby gets Dads:_____

Predictions

Eye Color: _____   Hair Color:_____

Length:_____   Weight:_____

D.O.B:_____   Time:_____

Labor will last: ___Days ___Hours ___Mins

Guests

Name:_____

Parenting Advice

_____
_____
_____
_____
_____
_____

Wishes for Baby

_____
_____
_____
_____
_____

Resemblance

☐ Mostly Mom   ☐ Definitely Dad

I hope the baby gets Moms:_____

I hope the baby gets Dads:_____

Predictions

Eye Color: _____   Hair Color:_____

Length:_____   Weight:_____

D.O.B:_____   Time:_____

Labor will last: ___Days ___Hours ___Mins

Gift log

Name: _____
Gift: _____
Thank You Sent: _____

Name: _____
Gift: _____
Thank You Sent: _____

Name: _____
Gift: _____
Thank You Sent: _____

Name: _____
Gift: _____
Thank You Sent: _____

Name: _____
Gift: _____
Thank You Sent: _____

Name: _____
Gift: _____
Thank You Sent: _____

Name: _____
Gift: _____
Thank You Sent: _____

Name: _____
Gift: _____
Thank You Sent: _____

Gift log

Name: _____
Gift: _____
Thank You Sent: _____

Name: _____
Gift: _____
Thank You Sent: _____

Name: _____
Gift: _____
Thank You Sent: _____

Name: _____
Gift: _____
Thank You Sent: _____

Name: _____
Gift: _____
Thank You Sent: _____

Name: _____
Gift: _____
Thank You Sent: _____

Name: _____
Gift: _____
Thank You Sent: _____

Name: _____
Gift: _____
Thank You Sent: _____

 Gift log

Name: _____
Gift: _____
Thank You Sent: _____

Name: _____
Gift: _____
Thank You Sent: _____

Name: _____
Gift: _____
Thank You Sent: _____

Name: _____
Gift: _____
Thank You Sent: _____

Name: _____
Gift: _____
Thank You Sent: _____

Name: _____
Gift: _____
Thank You Sent: _____

Name: _____
Gift: _____
Thank You Sent: _____

Name: _____
Gift: _____
Thank You Sent: _____

 Gift log

Name: _____
Gift: _____
Thank You Sent: _____

Name: _____
Gift: _____
Thank You Sent: _____

Name: _____
Gift: _____
Thank You Sent: _____

Name: _____
Gift: _____
Thank You Sent: _____

Name: _____
Gift: _____
Thank You Sent: _____

Name: _____
Gift: _____
Thank You Sent: _____

Name: _____
Gift: _____
Thank You Sent: _____

Name: _____
Gift: _____
Thank You Sent: _____

 Gift log

Name: _____
Gift: _____
Thank You Sent: _____

Name: _____
Gift: _____
Thank You Sent: _____

Name: _____
Gift: _____
Thank You Sent: _____

Name: _____
Gift: _____
Thank You Sent: _____

Name: _____
Gift: _____
Thank You Sent: _____

Name: _____
Gift: _____
Thank You Sent: _____

Name: _____
Gift: _____
Thank You Sent: _____

Name: _____
Gift: _____
Thank You Sent: _____

 Gift log

Name: _____
Gift: _____
Thank You Sent: _____

Name: _____
Gift: _____
Thank You Sent: _____

Name: _____
Gift: _____
Thank You Sent: _____

Name: _____
Gift: _____
Thank You Sent: _____

Name: _____
Gift: _____
Thank You Sent: _____

Name: _____
Gift: _____
Thank You Sent: _____

Name: _____
Gift: _____
Thank You Sent: _____

Name: _____
Gift: _____
Thank You Sent: _____

 Gift log

Name: _____
Gift: _____
Thank You Sent: _____

Name: _____
Gift: _____
Thank You Sent: _____

Name: _____
Gift: _____
Thank You Sent: _____

Name: _____
Gift: _____
Thank You Sent: _____

Name: _____
Gift: _____
Thank You Sent: _____

Name: _____
Gift: _____
Thank You Sent: _____

Name: _____
Gift: _____
Thank You Sent: _____

Name: _____
Gift: _____
Thank You Sent: _____

 Gift Log

Name: _____
Gift: _____
Thank You Sent: _____

Name: _____
Gift: _____
Thank You Sent: _____

Name: _____
Gift: _____
Thank You Sent: _____

Name: _____
Gift: _____
Thank You Sent: _____

Name: _____
Gift: _____
Thank You Sent: _____

Name: _____
Gift: _____
Thank You Sent: _____

Name: _____
Gift: _____
Thank You Sent: _____

Name: _____
Gift: _____
Thank You Sent: _____

 Gift log

Name: _____
Gift: _____
Thank You Sent: _____

Name: _____
Gift: _____
Thank You Sent: _____

Name: _____
Gift: _____
Thank You Sent: _____

Name: _____
Gift: _____
Thank You Sent: _____

Name: _____
Gift: _____
Thank You Sent: _____

Name: _____
Gift: _____
Thank You Sent: _____

Name: _____
Gift: _____
Thank You Sent: _____

Name: _____
Gift: _____
Thank You Sent: _____

 Gift log

Name: _____
Gift: _____
Thank You Sent: _____

Name: _____
Gift: _____
Thank You Sent: _____

Name: _____
Gift: _____
Thank You Sent: _____

Name: _____
Gift: _____
Thank You Sent: _____

Name: _____
Gift: _____
Thank You Sent: _____

Name: _____
Gift: _____
Thank You Sent: _____

Name: _____
Gift: _____
Thank You Sent: _____

Name: _____
Gift: _____
Thank You Sent: _____

 Gift log

Name: _____
Gift: _____
Thank You Sent: _____

Name: _____
Gift: _____
Thank You Sent: _____

Name: _____
Gift: _____
Thank You Sent: _____

Name: _____
Gift: _____
Thank You Sent: _____

Name: _____
Gift: _____
Thank You Sent: _____

Name: _____
Gift: _____
Thank You Sent: _____

Name: _____
Gift: _____
Thank You Sent: _____

Name: _____
Gift: _____
Thank You Sent: _____

 Gift log

Name: _____
Gift: _____
Thank You Sent: _____

Name: _____
Gift: _____
Thank You Sent: _____

Name: _____
Gift: _____
Thank You Sent: _____

Name: _____
Gift: _____
Thank You Sent: _____

Name: _____
Gift: _____
Thank You Sent: _____

Name: _____
Gift: _____
Thank You Sent: _____

Name: _____
Gift: _____
Thank You Sent: _____

Name: _____
Gift: _____
Thank You Sent: _____

Made in the USA
Monee, IL
04 March 2020